MARKED
BY YOUR HATRED

By the same Author:
toxic/empathy (2024)

before/after (2024)

Yellow Gerbera (2024) - A book of positive affirmations

Contributor: Foreword & Family History
Amusements of Solitude – 180ᵗʰ Anniversary Edition; *Alexander Herald* (2024)

Coming soon:
Sunshine: A little book of contemplative happiness (2025)

Content Note:
This collection contains themes of emotional and psychological abuse, gaslighting, trauma, and recovery. Some content may be distressing for readers who have experienced similar harm. Please take care while reading.

MARKED
BY YOUR HATRED

J L HERALD

Marked By Your Hatred

Copyright © 2025 JL Herald

All rights reserved.

This book or any portion thereof may not be reproduced or used in any manner whatsoever without the express written permission of the copyright owner, except for the use of brief quotations in a book review.

First Printed 2025
Australia

 A catalogue record for this work is available from the National Library of Australia

Cover Design © JL Herald 2025
Image © Aleksandr Goncharenko, Dreamtime Creations

ISBN: 978-0-6459915-7-4 (paperback)

Published by Yellow Gerbera Publications

Website: http://www.JLHerald-poet.com

For all the people

that have ever found themselves

standing in the rubble

of their trust,

their sanity,

and their safety

because of the actions

of someone they once cared about:

this book is for you.

PREFACE

This collection was born out of the ashes of a pain I was never meant to name. I was told again, and again, I was "not in control," that I was misremembering, exaggerating, or fabricating. For a long time, I lived in confusion, turmoil, and hurt—unravelling truths that kept slipping through my fingers. I doubted my own memory and myself. I was told the very words I had received in chat messages and emails were "fake," that I was making things up, and that I was delusional and obsessive. I was gaslit, manipulated, and burdened with guilt and shame that were never mine to carry.

Poetry became my sanctuary, a place where I could speak freely—without being silenced, without being attacked for telling the truth I knew in my bones was real.

Marked By Your Hatred is a record of my journey, but it's also the journey of so many others I've spoken with, cried with, and held hands with. Our stories echo one another: the same insidious tactics, the same disorienting fog, the same profound betrayal of trust and sense of self.

These poems are deeply rooted in psychological reality and research, exploring the processes of recognising and navigating toxic, emotionally and psychologically abusive relationships. I devoured books, articles, and blogs—anything I could find—desperate to understand the madness, to make sense of the senseless.

Some of the poems were written in anger, others through tears. Many found their form only after I finally discovered the language to articulate the slow, insidious erosion of my identity.

While this book stands on its own, it can also be read as a companion to my first book *toxic/empathy*, which explores earlier chapters of my experience.

I wrote this collection not only for myself, but for anyone who has ever doubted their own story because someone told them it didn't happen—even with absolute proof. For those who've been called too sensitive, too much, or too dramatic. For those falsely accused and driven to apologise for actions they never took—just to keep the peace. For those who lost their autonomy and voice through fear of repercussions. For those who stayed silent because it was safer to do so.

This is my voice.
This is their voice.
This is our truth.
And I no longer need anyone's permission to speak.

— **J.L. Herald**
August 2025

REALITY CAN
BE CRUELER THAN
ANYTHING YOUR
IMAGINATION
COULD CREATE

CONTENTS

PREFACE   7

FRACTURED
Monsters   15
Ouija Relationship   16
Gemini   19
Lighting Of The Gas   21
Puzzled   26
Testing   30
Windows To The Soul   32
Sorry   33
Malice   34
Jokes Of Misogyny   36
No Wasn't An Option   39
Dichotomy Of Reality   42
Psychosomatic   46
Final Foundation   47

MARKED
Come Close   51
Unwanted   52
Non-Fiction   54
Astral Stalking   55
Betrayed By Body Language   56
Erased   59
Judgement   63
You Wanted My Hate   65
I'm The Crazy One   67
The Path Of Love   68
She Stayed   70
Intellectually Raped   73
Broken Marble   74

SHATTERED

EXPECTATIONS	79
I CANNOT SPEAK	80
MANY WATCHERS	83
PORTMANTEAU	87
EVIL EYES	89
CATALOGUE OF EXCUSES	91
ENOUGH...NO MORE	94
MAIN CHARACTER SYNDROME	99
NEVER	101
CARROTS	102
UNFORGIVABLE	105
CREATIVE VAMPIRISM	106
THE FEAR INSIDE	107
DUFFTOWN	109
CRUMBLING REALITY	111

RECLAIMED

SAFE	115
YOUR NAME IS LIAR	117
CLARITY	120
GOD OF THE ABYSS	123
HOLLOW ECHOES	127
NO REGRETS	131
BALANCED	133
DROWNED BY INDIFFERENCE	136
THE CLIFF FACE ABOVE THE SEA	138
CONTROLLED	139
MARKED BY YOUR HATRED	141
I MOURNED YOU	142
BLIND	145
SMILE	147

AFTERWARD   151

NOTES   152

FRACTURED

MONSTERS

when we were young children the monsters we were told
were nasty evil creatures, wicked beings that are foul
we're told to avoid the strangers as monsters they might be
but never were we warned about the monsters that we see

you shouldn't be afraid of the monsters in the night
you should be afraid of the ones that douse your light
you shouldn't be afraid of the monsters of the deep
you should be afraid of the ones that watch you sleep

always being aware and scared of those that are unknown
we never stop to be afraid of the ones we call our own
the monsters that hide behind kind faces always smiling
the ones that we are told to trust their character beguiling

you shouldn't be afraid of the monsters in the skies
you should be afraid of the ones that shut your eyes
you shouldn't be afraid of the monsters in your mind
you should be afraid of the ones that close your blinds

we were always warned to be alert when going out
but never were we told to be afraid within our house
the monsters we are frightened of, they aren't the ones we meet
the monsters live within our sphere we are within their reach

you shouldn't be afraid of the monsters beneath your bed
you should be afraid of the ones that say they care
you shouldn't be afraid of the monsters in your closet
you should be afraid of the ones that say they love us

OUIJA RELATIONSHIP

"Jimi — JimBob," you said his name was,
considered to be—by you—one of your
closest friends, even though you saw him rarely.
well—that is what you kept telling me:
occasional emails and messages asking how you were,
catching up for dinner every couple of years,
from the time I started to get to know you,
in the dying days of twenty seventeen.

you fondly told me that your friendship was like
sliding into a prewarmed blanket—
like no time had passed when you were last
in the comforting bosom of his presence.

your very good friend Jimi
that you had dinner with in Sydney
one time during the COVID outbreaks—
and how you wished your friendships were like
the one you shared so comfortably:
talking semi-regularly,
but only catching up occasionally.

not like ours—
we used to chat almost daily,
our lives intertwined by stupid puns
and complaints about work and
idiots we encountered.

bike rides into far remote wilderness,
talks of future adventures
that might require helicopters.

but you kept comparing me to Jimi—
how we spoke too much—
and you wanted me to be
a friend like your friend Jimi.

yet again, near the end of everything,
part of me wondered if our friendship
might have been saved
if maybe I had been, as you described—
just a little more like
your very best friend, Jimi.

as our friendship morphed into hatred and spite,
I started to have to block you from my life.
I finally looked up Jimi—to build my fortress—
like all your friends whose names I remembered.

the surprise was a hit to the face with a spade,
while jamming a fork into a live outlet while smiling.

your friendship with Jimi
must have been through Ouija.
you stated so many times

that you wanted us to be a mirror
of the relationship you had with him—
but Jimi had died in twenty eighteen.

all those conversations, all those dinners,
must have occurred on some spectral plane
where Jimi now resided.
you wanted our friendship to be styled
like one you had with the deceased.

no wonder you got angry and frustrated with me—
I had not realised
that my dying
was a requirement
for our friendship to succeed.

GEMINI

within your mind, a split declared—
an arsehole's voice, a kind one's care.
the arsehole, sharp and quick to wound,
the kind one soft, and sought to soothe.

the arsehole made his loved one's crawl,
undermined and bruised them all.
the kind one tried to compensate,
with money, gifts—a sorry state.

you blamed it on your star-born sign,
a Gemini—with split design:
two voices clashing in your head,
unsure of right, unsure of dread.

but when the kind one shirked the blame,
"*it wasn't me — I'm not the same,*"
claimed no control, no conscious choice—
it wasn't truth, a coward's voice.

for both reside within one skin—
the harm, the guilt, the saint, the sin.
not two, but one, and when blood's spilled,
the kindly hands are just as filled.

you made excuses—tried to part
your fractured mind from fractured heart.
but you are he, and he is you—
you knew the harm—you saw it through.

don't blame the arsehole for your deeds,
the words you wrote, the spite you'd feed.
the kind one watched, then lent a hand—
you stood as one—you took a stand.

so don't pretend you were undone.
there aren't two people—only one
no alter ego took the fall—
the actions taken—they were yours.

LIGHTING OF THE GAS

he walks down darkened streets,
pausing at each lamppost
to light the gas—
illuminating the path
for her to follow.

she trails behind,
stopping to peer up at the flames,
the unique design of each lamp,
the beautiful scrollwork
flickering in the dark,
his voice explaining
the meaning of each swirl and stroke.

she marvels at the artistry—
each lamp a testament to his life,
and the trust in his truth
shared so easily
along the pathway he lit.

she glances back—
the street behind them
is wreathed in shadows.
no glow, no flame,
just endless deep darkness.

she touches his hand lightly,
gesturing behind.
"I never lit those,"
he says, calmly.
"you must be mistaken—
this is the only path we've taken."

and though her feet ache
from walking on cobblestones,
she remembers the details
of at least three lamps ago—
its shape and scrollwork
holding the glass.
she describes it in detail.
"no," he says.
"you're remembering it wrong.
there's no lamp like that
on this street—
maybe you saw it
some other time
with someone else."

he keeps walking,
but now he's silent
as he lights the lamps—
refusing to name their beauty

or describe their design.
"what's the point," he says,
"when you keep twisting things—
accusing me of bad things?"
she stutters, stops—
"but—I'm sure of what I saw.
that lamp—
you lit it."

he doesn't answer,
just moves to the next post,
striking a match
without looking at her.
her words hang in the air
like smoke—
was she really sure?

she wanders back,
but now the lamp seems different—
the scrollwork less ornate,
the glass not quite the same.
maybe she did remember it wrong.
his voice echoes—
inside her mind:
"see—you imagined it.

you twist things.
assumed things.
why would he lie?"

she turns again to see the lamps behind—
as one, just past the last crossroad,
sputters, flickering,
then fades to black.
"what are you talking about?" he says.
"there's no lamp there."

the next lamp
was beautifully lit from within
she takes a photo—
a memento,
something to remember him by.
he seems happier,
speaking again,
describing the lamp's design
and how he felt
as it was made and placed.
but when she mentions the story
he told just a moment before,
a little farther down
the same street—

he scoffs:
"what's wrong with you?
I never would have said that."

she shows him the photo—
a lit lamp,
engraving at the base
clearly showing his name.

"that's fake," he mutters.
"why would you show me that?
look again—
that lamp isn't there—
it never happened,
you're imagining it."

she blinks at the image,
then at the darkened street—
confusion etched in her eyes.

something inside her
whispers:
"you were right.
weren't you?"

PUZZLED

a small piece with tabs and blanks—
a partial image of yourself—
handed over during dinner conversation,
at that restaurant called *Sage*,
laid between wine glasses
and tiny flower garnishes.

another piece followed,
slightly grey, with an orange splash through it,
offered on an e-bike ride
outside a hut on the side of a mountain—
reflecting the faded red door
of the hut we explored—
the pieces' colour was unexpected,
its edges slightly frayed.

I turned it over in my hands,
noticing how it didn't fit with the others—
the ones I had so far collected—
but I kept it anyway,
waiting for the picture to reveal itself.

I never received pieces to form the edge,
never did I glimpse a corner.
no frame to anchor my unease,
which crept like a cockroach
as things stopped making sense—

just a growing pile of middle bits,
each one insisting it had meaning.

sometimes the pieces clicked,
fitting together to make a slightly bigger image.
my inner voice sighing *ooooh*.
a smile matching a childhood story,
a laugh that echoed a shared inside joke—
like the Kosciuszko yellow lines
we argued over halfway between
Thredbo and Jindabyne,
and that emoji we called poo finger—
me reading too much
into a silly image and what you might have meant—
and for a moment,
the picture expanded.

but there were too many gaps,
odd voids where nothing belonged.
holes shaped like truths
you never handed over.
a burgeoning feeling
that you didn't make sense.

then came the pieces that poured
in the box I stored them,
while we were in New Zealand—
a handful, offered in haste,

edges worn by overuse,
bent and missing tabs—
bits of truth with
essential joiners missing.

others didn't match the tone or hue,
completely mismatching
everything I already had
and the picture on the box I held.
they felt foreign,
like they belonged to another life,
another person,
another box entirely.

and yet you insisted:
they're part of me,
the real me.

you said I was building the puzzle wrong—
that I'd been imagining someone else
this whole time
placing pieces where they never belonged
that some of the pieces were never yours.

but I was using the box you gave me,
with the picture you painted with words,
the image you curated—
with soft smiles.

select memories—
and anger
that I would even dare question.

how could I be clicking the wrong puzzle
when I was only working with pieces you supplied—
your clues, your fragments?

I sat with it all,
spread across the floor,
hands aching from sorting,
trying to join pieces that didn't fit,
eyes sore from searching
for meaning in my confusion.

I sought clarity, a better image—
you declared
I didn't have any right to your picture,
as I hadn't earnt the privilege.

your puzzle was unsolvable.
an impossibility with no edges,
clashing images and
too many pieces that
just never matched—
you left me puzzled on purpose.

TESTING

he crafted small traps to test her will,
to see the moment her warmth turned chill—
a slip of words, designed to degrade,
to watch if she would break or fade.
one day was friendly, the next one mean,
to test if she'd stay soft and keen.
he'd twist her smile into a wince,
then count the seconds until she flinched.

she'd question her feelings, "am I too much?"
blaming her nature, each tender touch.
if he was unkind, she'd search for blame,
a whispered fault she'd dare not name.
she'd question all she said or showed,
wondering if she'd made him cold.
her deep conviction, sharp and cruel—
that she had caused his sudden chill.

he told cruel jokes—would she laugh or freeze?
stayed silent for days—to see if she'd plead.
manipulated her emotions to see if she'd break,
pulling and pushing to watch her ache.
he played with guilt like a loaded gun,
claimed she was selfish, or else "no fun."
if she pushed back, he'd change his face—
act tender again, then vanish in place.

each step towards him, a silent dread,
a question mark hanging over her head.
would gentle words greet, or eyes turn cold?
a story of mercy, or rage untold?
she practiced her smile, her voice soft and low,
never quite certain which way winds would blow.
then, a flicker of ease, a fragile release,
when his face turned to smile, bringing fleeting peace.

he played cruel games to gain her trust,
he fed on her hope and labelled it lust.
if she kept coming back, he'd tighten the bind—
each return a signal: "she's nearly mine."
and when at last she ceased to resist,
he smiled, concluding she passed his test.
not love, not care—just keep her from leaving
he bonded her love with cruel deceiving.

WINDOWS TO THE SOUL

when I gazed into the depths of

eyes coloured like whiskey

I had thought to find warmth—

a soul worth wrapping myself in.

but the eyes were broken

jagged shards that pierced

empty echoes within a derelict abode—

the slow, decaying rot of termites

eating at the morals

and remains

of your already dying soul.

SORRY

was it me?
did I really do that?
was I wrong?
I didn't mean to—
I didn't mean to upset you.
I tried not to.
was it me?

has my memory betrayed me?
have the lines blurred—
between what happened
and what you said happened?

I'm sorry.
for all the things I did.
for all the things I might have done.
for making you unhappy.

it must have been me, right?
you said you'd never hurt me.
you said I was family.
and family doesn't lie—
not when looking me in the eye.

so it must be me.
it has to be me.
I must be wrong.

I'm sorry—
not just for what I did,
but for not even knowing
what it was
I did.

MALICE

malice (noun) *ma-les:*
the desire to cause pain or distress to another

    I held your message like a fragile glass—
    "you need to know what I've done
    was never with malice."
    but why shatter silence unbidden?
    what hidden poison drips beneath your words—
    a serpent coiled, waiting in the shadow?
    what secret storms stir behind your smile?
    why did you send this text?
    had I overlooked the weeds in your garden—
    unaware of the thorns you sharpened,
    the vines that twisted quietly,
    waiting to strangle me unawares?

malicious (adjective) *me-'li-shes,*
having or showing harm to someone

    if you knew you'd been nasty—
    saying things unkind,
    making me out to be delusional or crazy—
    if you knew it would devastate me—
    and still chose to say or do
    whatever it was—
    do you understand that is what
    the dictionary definition
    of what malice is?

malevolence (noun) *me-'le-ve-len(t)s:*
the quality or state of having, or showing intense ill will,
spite, or hatred

    you cast stones into my quiet lake,
    knowing ripples would drown me—
    knowing every splash was corrosive acid.
    no shadows were twisting your arm
    threatening you harm.
    still, you hurled your stones,
    then begged me to believe
    your actions were pure—
    even as you made me look deranged.
    you needed to tell me, for whatever reason
    that you never,
    ever did them with malice.

    bullshit.

JOKES OF MISOGYNY

"what's one plus one?" he liked to ask,
as if it were a test.
she'd say "it's two"—he'd sigh, then scoff,
like she'd failed some sacred quest.

he wasn't seeking answers, no—
just a scene to stage his act.
a woman who could *add?* absurd!
that's not a female fact.

a uterus? poor girl was doomed,
too weighted down to think.
perhaps her thoughts got tangled up
in hormone-laden pink.

he dubbed it "logic" when he spoke,
that smug and sacred word.
but logic died the day he thought
he was the smartest in the herd.

testosterone, his magic fuel—
as a penis grants such flair
on science, space, and how, of course,
he knew more than all the bears

she challenged him—imagine that! —
and named the creeping rot.
"misogyny," she dared to say,
which proved she'd lost the plot.

"relax," he said. "it's just a joke.
don't take things so to heart."
because, you see, when men offend,
it's basically performance art.

just lads being lads, around the fire,
with beer and witless grace—
while every joke they cracked that night
was aimed right at her face.

he didn't know she came from queens
of numbers, stars, and bones—
women who cracked the code of life
while he still googled tunes.

three PhDs? impressive, sure—
but can they open jars?
who needs the facts when he's equipped
with barbecues and cars?

she mapped out steps with patient calm,
each formulae precise—
he nodded like he understood,
then mansplained his own advice.

to him, she was an air-filled toy,
with curves and cheerful moans—
an amazon deal, shipped overnight,
with holes where thoughts should go.

and still he said she lacked the wit,
the humour, and delight—
though he confused his own reflection
for a man who might be right.

he thought she was the joke—poor soul—
but here's the painful twist:
the only punchline in the room
was swinging between his hips.

NO WASN'T AN OPTION

I lay on the grass
in the quiet outside Lutons crutching shed
at the far southern border of Namadgi
clouds high above Gudgenby,
towering Mt Kelly, a silent sentinel.

we had agreed to be just friends—
friends that took bike rides
in remote places of the ACT—
just friends—you insisted and I agreed.

I liked you—liked talking to you
but no longer saw you sexually
not in a while,
months—maybe years.

I was not expecting
the darkening
of my sun.

we had a boundary —
your words, my words,
a line drawn in trust.
you kept crossing it,
stepping over what we'd both agreed.

I didn't have a choice —
lying on the grass,
the breeze on my arms,

your weight on my will.
you never asked or checked
whether what you wanted
was something I wanted too.

your tongue was in my mouth
your hand grasping at
the band around my waist
clutching, gripping
moving—
sliding.

I closed my eyes and gave in
I disappeared within
my muscles slackened—
to avoid escalation.

we were alone out there—
my mind crying no
but my mouth unable to speak it,
as past dissents about anything
resulted in threats of non-friendship,
cold silences,
consequences I would not like,
or the possibility of something
deeply unsaid.

so, I lay there in the open
the kangaroos grazing
distantly—unaware
while you trampled all over
our mutually agreed boundary.

then later:
you said—
    I wanted more than friendship,
that—
    I kept pushing boundaries,
that—
    I made you uncomfortable
    with demands of sexual things.
even when I never did.

as if
no
was ever
an option.

DICHOTOMY OF REALITY

(to his friends)
I met a new girl—she's amazing and wild,
she talks like a dream and glows when she smiles.
she makes little pendants in elvish and runes,
dreams of travels beneath foreign moons.
she's quirky, creative, a little out there,
dresses with corsets and a cape with flair
she's different, unique—I like her energy
I think I've found someone to create some memories.

(to her)
you're such a lovely person to be near,
my favourite voice I long to hear.
our silly chats—I wait all day,
you make the dark thoughts go away.
you calm my storms with every word,
you're revealing things I've never heard.
I hope you know this bond is rare—
I miss you, even when you're there.

(to his friends)
this girl—she's obsessed—won't leave me alone,
she's texting too much, she's glued to her phone.
she shows up near places she shouldn't be,
it's like she's addicted, she's harassing me.
I've told her it's done, I've made that clear,
but she keeps popping up—she's so fucking weird.
I don't know how to make her stop—
her fixation's turning into a ticking clock.

(to her)
I'm so happy that we're friends, you see—
you're the only one who gets all of me.
I've spent my life avoiding ties,
but with you, I'm learning not to disguise.
let's book a trip, escape the grey,
to an island where troubles melt away.
you mean more than I can say—
you're my safest place in any day.

(to his friends)
this girl is mental, she's out of control,
telling wild stories—she's dug a dark hole.
if she says I hurt her, she's making it up,
just looking for drama to stir the cup.
she gives me the creeps, I can't stand her face,
I avoid her like plague—get me out of this place.
I need her gone, I can't pretend—
god, when will this madness end?

(to her)
let's catch up soon for whisky and talk,
we'll sit by the fire, go out for a walk.
we'll plan new adventures, just you and I,
you're family to me—I'd hate goodbye.
you always make me smile, you know—
that's rare for me, it doesn't show.
you've made this loner feel brand new—
I hope this bond will always be true.

(her)
which one was real, and which was lie?
the warmth in your eyes or the cold goodbye?
were you my friend, as you claimed with pride,
or just a mask that you wore to hide?
did you love me or loathe me—tell me true,
were the kind words fake? was I a fool to you?
your messages clash with what others heard—
which one of you spoke an honest word?

(to his friends)
this girl is fixated, she walks past my place,
I'm scared she's unstable—she stares into space.
if she kills my dogs, I won't be shocked,
she's twisted inside, like a mind that's blocked.
she's calling me cruel, she's making up lies,
telling the world I wore abuse as disguise.
I don't know why, she's fucking deranged—
I just want this nightmare changed

(to her)
you know you're unwell, you've crossed a line,
the things you've said aren't yours to define.
you're stalking, obsessing—it's not okay,
you need some help to stay away.
I've tried to be kind, I've tried to stay near,
but now I feel nothing but pity and fear.
you've built a story that just isn't true—
you're sick, and I can't keep helping you.

(her)
I've been nowhere near, not once, not now—
I kept my distance—your anger taught me how.
your words are here in black and white,
I've saved your texts, they shine like light.
I've printed them out—each promise, each plea,
the "forever friends" you swore we'd be.
I haven't stalked, I haven't lied—
you're rewriting me from the outside.

(to his friends)	*(to her)*
she's lying	you're lying
you see it	I know it
she's unwell	you're unwell
out of control	out of control

(her)
…. am I?

PSYCHOSOMATIC

the ECG monitors beeped
tracing the slowly breaking
heart.

she had seen him that day—
stressed and wary—
watching the words that she thought,
moulding and modifying
before she said anything.

he still had not taken it well.

next time, she thought—
next time I'll say it differently—
or maybe not at all.

next time came,
and next time went.

her days ending with
pains around her heart,
an arm she couldn't feel,
a dizzy disassociation
between her mind and her body.

each time laying
staring at the clinical white,
monitors on her chest
tracing and watching
her slowly dying heart.

FINAL FOUNDATION

it was a Tuesday—
just a bit before the last work stragglers arrived
when the final foundation crumbled.
I was typing up some requirements
sipping my latte made with the juice of a nut
while a silent missile was being prepped
for the explosion
in the bay next to me.

your name was spoken in the hushed tones
by someone that cares about the sanctity of office space,
the first time in more than twelve months
the syllables of your name
assaulted my eardrums.

I froze.

the strawberry iced donut I ate that morning
decided to pay another visit to my mouth,
the colour of my face draining—
spilling onto my document.
I have to tell them.
I stood in that tiny meeting room
at the side of the building like a fish in a bowl.

glass walls.
exposed.
nothing to hide behind.

I had been under the illusion that others respected you.
I had kept quiet, and never said anything
as I did not want dig under your foundations
even after you had tried to topple mine.

arrogant.
difficult to work with.
suffers from main person syndrome.
blackmailed by undecipherable coding.
whatthefuck.

they spoke about your permanency—
of the team you worked in, not a team you led.
one hundred and eighty degrees out of phase
from what you had whispered in my being,
you weren't what you had said
at the very beginning.

my confusion vomited up more questions
but answers were elusive,
I was speaking another language
as my version of you
and their version
didn't match up and didn't make sense.

I was left standing in the rubble—
the foundation you had given
nothing but ashes and dust.

MARKED

COME CLOSE

please look into my eyes

and stroke my lovely hair

I'm really very friendly

come visit me, I dare

I promise I won't hurt you

I promise I'll be nice

but I think you know me far too well

as all I say to you is lies

UNWANTED

it was just a little notification
displayed at the top of the AMOLED
screen of my Samsung S23:

> 10:43PM
>
> Friend Request Received

unwanted, unneeded, and unlooked for.
a request by a person I never wanted to see.
a coiling snake of anxiety
unwinding itself within my belly
a whispering hiss: *"what if it's him?"*
fifteen months of silence had preceded
a shattering second.

> 10:45PM
>
> I am still watching

indecision and confusion
make war
inside the slowly unravelling
ball of safety,
upending the fragile feeling
that I had finally been free.

it was she—the flying monkey
maybe looking for answers
maybe trying to explain
the confusion.

do I, or don't I?

benefit of doubt
given like a present
wrapped in old newspapers—
the faintest hope
that maybe you came with kindness
but my belief fizzled like
a match in a storm.

it was a violation of my person.
my privacy—an illusion,
my hope:
    dragged out.
    kidnapped.
    gagged.
    and murdered.

I will never be free.

NON-FICTION

I read a little book today—
I heard it was a hoot
a little book of non-fiction
about ex-lovers and their feud.
I am a fan of history
I read those front to back
of Romans and Egyptian gods
cataloguing all the facts.

it was an interesting title
the book written in your name
it detailed all the actions
to which I was held acclaim.
some people read aloud for me
and advised me of distress
I had to totally agree with them
the main character is a mess.

this little book, I have to say
if I read it without knowledge
I would too, find hatred there
the protagonist needs a wallop.
alas! I had to rate one star
the book—it was just awful
although it said it was non-fiction
that book—it was a novel.

ASTRAL STALKING

as I was in bed, sleepy, my eyes getting droopy
I started practicing astral projection
since you had implied, I was out of my mind
my body had slipped your detection.

the only way I could be where you stated you'd seen
me outside of your marked habitation
is if somehow I'd known how to let go of my soul
and sent it to haunt your location.

somehow while sleeping—I was driving and creeping
watching you as you walked your hounds.
when I was in dreamland—my being was screaming
obscenities at the edge of your grounds.

keeping you wide awake with my ghostly white face
floating dramatically outside on the street.
as I haven't been in the town where you live—
I must have stalked you while I was asleep.

BETRAYED BY BODY LANGUAGE

the very last time I had the misfortune
to see you—outside courtroom four
that place you had dragged me to—
I don't think you quite understood
just what you had done.
it's one thing to spin bullshit
into your girlfriend's ear,
or weave sagas of hardship
for the captive sympathy
of friends and family—
but once you step through
those revolving doors of law,
your words must be the truth—
or risk perjury.

you knew that. well, I think you did.

I never worked out what your end game was
did you think it clever—
calling me to the stand
as if I'd help you take me down?

after all—I brought receipts:
photographs,
thousands of messages,
emails you sent,
statutory declarations from others

about the things that you did.
even after you claimed
everything I had was fiction,
pure fabrication,
you knew—
authenticity doesn't spew your kind of hatred.

your statements read like
the collected works of the Brothers Grimm
as you could not look at me—not once—
even when I addressed you directly.

you stared anywhere but my face,
answering with averted eyes,
fabricating,
stitching together a narrative
that never belonged to me.

you always told stories
like they were acts of service—
lies offered as gifts,
wrapped in plausible concern.
but the truth doesn't tremble like that.
it doesn't shift its weight,
doesn't flinch
when I finally looked you in the face.

you wore your suit like a disguise—
as if dressing the part

might rewrite the lines
you'd rehearsed in your mind.
but your suit was as ill-fitting
as the narrative you dreamt up.

I lost years believing you.
building a connection on fault lines
you quietly carved beneath my feet.
but when I stood outside that courtroom
I stood steady—
        and you *cracked*.

in that moment your body betrayed you
confessing to what I had already known—
what your mouth had tried to bury—
what your words twisted and blurred.
for the first time
you finally understood:
I was no longer afraid of you—
I would no longer let you
question my memory
or allow seeds of doubt to flourish.
I no longer believed you—
or wanted a single thing to do with you.
and I?

I had the means
to take your bullshit
apart.

ERASED

you took an eraser to history
with wide, brutal swipes
through memory—
removing
what didn't suit your story anymore.
two weeks in New Zealand?
deleted.
all those bike rides through Kosciuszko?
faded and sepiaed—
like old files
you dragged to trash
and never looked back.
no photos. no tags.
no trace.
I don't even show up
in your memories folder.

it was easy for you to delete me.
even when we were happening,
in the moment
living it—
you had already cut me out
I wasn't in your stories.

you—the lone hero,
hacking through undergrowth,
scaling mountains,
riding solo,

posting captions like:
"just me, out here,
doing it all on my own."

except—
I was there.
always there.
on a bike next to you.
hiking up that mountain with you.
behind the phone,
sending you coordinates.
researching the where, and the how.
devising the plans.
backing up your every
'spontaneous' moment.
while you just threw
money at me.
and now?
the messages—gone.
the photos—denied.
erased.

you took eighteen months
and compressed them into
eight inconsequential weeks.
fragmented the timeline
until I was unrecognisable—
a ghost
wandering your deleted scenes.

you needed it that way.
you needed the space
to rewrite the past
without contradiction,
to narrate a version
where I was never a chapter—
just a misplaced page
you tore out
before handing your story
to an audience
who would only believe you.

to show me I was never
ever important.

now I am just—
a null result.
a line of corrupted code.
a cached memory never mentioned.
a stupid,
forgotten, never there
idiot
whose only mistake
was believing—
that love and care
was something you'd cherish.

believing that data
was proof you couldn't deny:

the messages in Hangouts
silly puns shared in Signal
thousands of millions
of interactions
photos of fun—
over five years of your life.

I wonder—
how do you convince yourself
so thoroughly
that I never mattered?
that nothing we did ever happened?

that you could just...

delete.

JUDGEMENT

he sat - silently staring
as the judge considered glaring
as it became slowly evident
that he was there without a clue.
it was starting to become clear:
he was totally without care,
hadn't read the words supplied,
and had turned up unawares.

the judge—he left the chambers
to consider legal tomes.
her legal argument rang true,
the outcome was unknown.
he refused to look at her,
avoiding her gaze—instead to stare
at anything but her being—
as he knew what she'd been seeing.

he knew that he'd been lying,
that his evidence was dying,
and she wasn't behaving
like the times he made her scared.
she wasn't listening to the crap—
the mistruths and lights of gas,
the written lies of his bullshit
that had fallen out of his trap.

so when he opened up his mouth
to argue with the judge,
it became far more apparent
that intelligence was not much.
pile of papers stacked sky high—
casually rifled through, aside—
more than half a ream of paper,
yet no words had been applied.

he'd tried to give impression
that he had lots of evidence,
but empty paper white
showed a presence full of spite.
thus all that was proven
was that he was a total loser,
as his blank pages of stupidity
just proved mediocrity.

YOU WANTED MY HATE

you wanted me to hate you—
that's what logic told me,
whispering in my ear late at night
as I lay cocooned in safety,
chasing sheep that kept avoiding me

you offered up shiny trinkets of possibility,
wrapped in layers of pretty opinion—
trips overseas,
helicopters in Tasmania,
fancy dinners and whisky in Barton.

but you said you never said
you'd actually do those,
did you?

you pushed me,
then pulled me back
every time I had made the choice
to walk away—cut you off.
messages would appear with
promises you never once made good on.
you convinced me holding you to them
was bullying you with your own words.

was I really wrong?
was it really me?

I wondered, again, and again,
feeling the tightening knot of frustration,
and the slow, cold burn
of resentment.

because you wanted me to hate you—
choose to walk away.
then you could look at others
with hurt and pain in your eyes:
"I didn't do anything to her.
I don't understand why she says
I did bad things.
I supported her. I cared.
now she's treating me
like I'm her ex.
her past has caught up
spewing its vomit on me."

you wanted me to hate you.
you got what you asked for—
me out of your life,
never wanting to know you,
while you pretended to be wounded,
so others would pity you
and look upon me with derision.

you wanted me to hate you—
but you failed.
there's no feeling left at all.

I'M THE CRAZY ONE

you needed me broken—the one out of place,
a being whose own mind they couldn't embrace.
you needed the chaos, that loss of control,
so my truth—when revealed—would take a dark toll.
you said that you love and you said that you care,
while telling all others I was mentally impaired.
well look at me now, standing tall, standing smart,
lighting a fire in the absolute dark.
your games are all over, evil spells are undone—
the 'crazy one' has only just truly begun.
my voice now unbroken has loudly proclaimed:
the real madness here was always your name.

so, who's really crazy? who's making up lies?
who's rewriting history with a clever disguise?
who took eighteen months and turned it to weeks?
who is making allegations about things I never did?
as I wasn't crazy—I cut your access,
you couldn't believe it—you thought me obsessed.
you said I was needy, you said I was mad,
said I twisted the truth to make you sound bad.
you said I was heartless, that I didn't care,
you claimed I was stalking—but I wasn't there.
so who's really crazy? Who's lost their control?
I know it's not me—it's reality you stole.

THE PATH OF LOVE

he called it love—
that everything he did
was because he followed
his path of love.

does love lie?
does love speak words of kindness
and words of disgust at the same time?
does love guide to confuse—
having others lose themselves
in the misdirection you force them through—
leading them down a path
that ends only in disappointment,
in a hall of mirrors
that no longer shows their own reflection?

does love confound?
does love say one thing
while speaking something else?
does love take your hand
and insist on steps designed to trip you—
forcing ridicule and scorn when you fall,
as you were meant to—
because happiness was
was always out of reach,
as the goalposts kept moving?

does love hurt?
does love come with sharpened blades
that slice off pieces of another?
does love demand that reality
is only what he says—
where the words said last week
or written today don't exist,
and memory is overwritten
with fog and falsehoods
he manufactured?

why is his path of love
an overgrown trail
littered with rocks and weeds
and unstable foundations?

he called it love—
but why does his path
look so much like a path of hate?

SHE STAYED

she stayed because of the flowers
he brought when they first started dating—
when it appeared he listened,
and she hoped he'd remember how.

she stayed for the promises
of future adventures
that never came,
though he kept talking about them.

she stayed because every time
she thought of leaving—
one foot out the door—
the man he used to be
would reappear
with kind words, shared plans,
compliments just enough
to make her pause.

she stayed for their history,
the moments he wouldn't let her forget—
all the good times,
how much he had loved her then,
how much he'd appreciated her—
but no longer did.

she stayed because she believed him
when he promised not to hurt her—
even as he did.

she stayed because she thought
if she told him he was hurting her—
he'd stop.

she stayed because she believed his words
and ignored the actions
that made those words meaningless.

she stayed, even after she started
keeping count—
of the lies,
the bruises no one could see,
the hours she spent convincing herself
she was the problem.

she stayed because she hoped.

she stayed because she dreamed.

she stayed because she was told
her mind was broken,
that she needed help.

she stayed because she couldn't imagine
a life without his direction,
because he'd convinced her
she wasn't capable
of thinking for herself.

she stayed
because she lost herself,
trying to make sure
he stayed happy.

she stayed,
until there was nothing
left
of her
to stay.

INTELLECTUALLY RAPED

he knew her boundaries—red lines, clearly drawn,
what she would not permit, what must be withdrawn.
she'd made no secret of what she despised—
so he played the part and stayed in the lines.

but he lied—he still did what she feared the most.
he craved her closeness, so he buried his ghost.
he claimed to honour the rules she had set,
but thought: if she finds out, i'll lose my access.

so he masked his truth—but still did what she hated.
his smiles were practiced, his lines calculated.
what he stole wasn't lawful—it twisted her will,
an intellectual rape, a consent he could kill.

he slipped through the gate to her inner sanctum,
fully aware that the truth would have banned him.
he took away her sacred right to choose
who may be let in, and who to refuse.

it's not your right to be allowed to deceive,
to sidestep someone else's stated needs.
to take what is guarded through calculated lies
it is still rape—no matter how you justify.

BROKEN MARBLE

you saw me from afar—
a marble Aphrodite: cold, untouchable,
chipped and stained by time
and the hands of past admirers.
you lingered, distant,
until I beckoned:
come see me. I'm not broken,
not as damaged as you think.

you embraced me—so I thought—
my little cracks and flaws
made me more interesting, more alive.
less like a sacred statue,
more like you—or so you said.
you saw my cracks and papered over them,
kissed them in the moonlight,
said they made my light shine.

I didn't see the chisel in your hand,
the mallet hidden in your smile.

it started small—just a swipe of sandpaper,
smoothing a section you said was "off."
tweak this, trim that—
just small adjustments to make me "better."
tiny slivers lost,
parts you insisted I didn't need.
just to make me more attractive.

you spoke of polish, of making me shine,
but the rag you used was soaked in acid,
eating at my foundation.

you didn't stop at the surface.
you found the cracks I already carried—
hairline fractures from time and grief—
slid your chisel into each one,
calling them faults I needed to fix.
you said you were helping me heal,
making me worthier,
so others would like me more.
but healing shouldn't feel like destruction
fixing shouldn't start with demolition.

you widened what was manageable,
turned scars into chasms,
sculpted shame where memory once lived.
and when I crumbled beneath your hands,
you blamed the marble
too soft,
too flawed to sculpt properly.

you left me shattered—
a pile of fragments where a goddess once stood.
no longer whole,
just pieces scattered,
a broken soul.

SHATTERED

EXPECTATIONS

overwhelmed by others' pleas
expectations of who I should be
too many versions, too much me
ripped apart for others' needs
I don't know who or what they want
I only know that I am not enough
the person that I know I am
is lost amongst others' demands

I CANNOT SPEAK

the hesitation—
a stutter inside
placing a barrier
preventing my tongue
wrapping itself around
what has been bouncing
around the synapses
like static—
for weeks.

"I'm not happy"

the heart and the mind
have been in conference
over coffee
and whisky discussing
how to birth a sentence
without bleeding for it.

"I'm worried about his reaction"

the heart whispers: "be honest."
the brain retorts: "be safe."
arguments daily
over syllables,
syntax,
and how to wrap my hurt
in something more palatable.

"If it's not said in the right way—
 he will get angry"

so—
I say nothing.
and for that silence?
I get a reward.
a compliment.
a promise for something.
a possibility of a future activity
if I say nothing.
but the disquiet—grows
like weeds in a garden
no one tends to anymore.

"I'm uneasy, I'm not sure I want this anymore"

he asks—
"are you okay?"
and I nod—
a puppet
with glass eyes,
and a marionette smile,
while inside me—
a war presses pause
mulling over the consequences
he promised
if I didn't do what he wanted.

disturbing the peace
comes with problems
far greater
than exposing my feelings.

always met with
hostility —
and my apologies
for feelings I hadn't even yet voiced.

so I stay quiet.

I cannot speak.

MANY WATCHERS

    she scans
public places—
      hurries through.
     places he once visited.

      just in case.

    he said he is watching.
     always watching.
      many others
       watching.

     nowhere is safe.
       under surveillance—
       he is watching.
      always
       watching.
     waiting for her.
     eyes on her,
      many
     eyes
       on her.

    watching.
    many watchers.

don't use
  social media
    he's watching.
   fake names.
  other accounts.
    many are his...

          watching
always watching

  asking others
     to look.
        unknown
           friends—
         acquaintances—
      strangers.
        watching.
           always watching.

    many watchers.

google
  a recipe—
    he says he
      can see
        sites she visited
          last week
           watching.
              always watching.

send
 an email—
   he can
    see that too.
     tracing
    conversations.

       watching.
          always watching.

friend request
　　from his partner:
　　　　confirmation:
　　he's watching.
　　　　always watching.

　confessions his friends
　　are watching.
months
　of
　　watching.
　　　　many watchers.

　　　walk
　　　　down
　　　　　the street.
cars
　passing—
　　some
　　　slow.
　　mind
　　　freezes.
　　a van.
　　　a bearded man.
　　　　watching.
　　　　　always watching.

cars
　outside
　　her house.
　people
　　taking
　　　photographs.

why are they?
　　who are they?

　　　　are they—
　　　　　　watching?

　　always watching.

many watchers.

　　　　　　　　　　　　nowhere is safe.

PORTMANTEAU

the cool white cotton whispered
as she lay staring
at the expanse of white
over her head
a portmanteau of blame
resting on the floor
near her feet.

It had been packed and repacked—
the parts she owned,
plainly labelled and left out,
ensuring none of hers
had been tetrised into what obviously wasn't.

she posted his—
the sticker had his name clearly printed—
but she received it back
with a note: "not mine."

he had stuffed more in,
so much more
that the sides bulged
and the zip would not close.

she carefully reviewed each item,
contemplating whether maybe
she had been mistaken—
slicing off things that might have been,

or could have been hers,
even if she was no longer sure.
the pile of hers grew larger,
and the pile of his,
still within the portmanteau, smaller.

she re-sent via express,
but it came back—almost instantly
with the words scribbled hastily on the outside:
"return to sender: name not known at this address."

EVIL EYES

I looked evil in the eyes
as it told me that it cared,
and I gave it my trust
as my soul – I laid it bare.

I looked evil in the eyes
as it told me of its love,
our relationship was worthy
and it'll always put us above.

I looked evil in the eyes
as it spoke of us forever,
I gave it all my love
and faced the world together.

I looked evil in the eyes
as it stroked me with its glove,
and I gave it my heart
like a broken little dove.

I looked evil in the eyes
as it went behind my back,
destroying my good name
telling others I was cracked.

I looked evil in the eyes
as its words revealed lies,
and the promises that were broken
showed the emptiness inside.

I looked evil in the eyes
until evil looked back at me,
and I saw that it hated—
finally saw what it sees.

I looked evil in the eyes
as the mask finally dropped
and realised that this evil
never once loved me for me.

CATALOGUE OF EXCUSES

she kept a book in the section between fiction
and non-fiction in the catalogue of titles
within the filing cabinets within her head—
never quite sure where it belonged—
this book she had crudely scribbled on: "why."

the pages were loose and well-used,
dog-eared with folded corners,
as if those pages had been pulled out
and examined for flaws and inconsistencies.
highlighter—faded pink in places—bled across
certain words in paragraphs:
"you made me,"
"you're confusing me with someone else,"
"your assumptions caused this argument."

stains of dried-out tears marred
the crinkled, worn, yellowed pages,
smearing the ink:
"this wouldn't have happened if you kept your opinions to yourself,"
"I just wanted you be nice to me,"
"you're too emotional,"
"you always overthink things."

she annotated the paragraphs,
squashed notes into the margins,
barely legible
as she tried to understand:

maybe I misunderstood.
he didn't mean it the way it sounded.
he's just had a shit day at work.
I shouldn't have asked him how he was.
I should know how to say things right.

on the inner cover,
she sketched rough tables—
noting her learnings,
things to implement, and maybe—
just maybe—
she could show she was improving:

why bringing up bad things he did is wrong.
why I should try harder to make him happy.
why I need to be better next time.
why I'm not worthy.

she logged incidents in a separate index—
cross-referencing chapters—
'apologies' with 'what he said I did,'
trying to decode what lesson
she had failed to learn.

the chapters grew longer over time—
pages filled with apologies
she had written in advance,
ready to offer without being asked.

sometimes she caught herself
grabbing for the book,
searching for something to appease him
as she'd stumbled over her wording.

and yet—
despite the pages and pages of reasons,
so many excuses and justifications
on why she was the problem,
why she was unworthy,
why she needed to earn his love—
she always returned to the very first page
contemplating the first note
she had scrawled in haste
when the book was brand new—
faded, smudged, and barely legible:

if he cared, why does he hurt?

ENOUGH...NO MORE

he looked at the body
lying prone on the floor
beaten and bloody,
clothing all torn
she smiled at him then,
her face twisted in pain
laughed out loud lightly,
in a soft breath she said:

> "you think your mistreatment
> was righteous and just,
> that your beliefs and your thoughts
> were ones I could trust.
> you never once realised
> never connected the dots—
> the truths you projected
> were never my thoughts.
> you've beaten, you've torn
> you've ripped me apart,
> for things I never did
> and thoughts I never thought.
>
> I'm done now, it's over,
> I've finally had enough,
> look in the mirror, boy—
> you think you're so tough
> the voices inside you—
> speaking for me—

weren't ever my thoughts,
they weren't ever me."

she crawled to the door,
a wince pressed on her lips,
tears traced down her cheek—
the scars of conflict.
she pulled herself up,
a deep breath in her chest,
placed her hand on the lever,
and softly confessed:

"you know I once loved you
I longed for your smile,
but everything that happened
shows I was in denial.
you did not ever
want me to succeed,
you only cared about
your own selfish needs.
if I got in the way
you'd decide to tear down,
watched me defend you
while you let me drown.

I wanted your happiness
to feel content
but you never wanted me

to feel what I dreamt.
every time I climbed higher
you'd create a new fight—
false accusations
just to prove you were right.
you hated that others
liked me so much better;
that my drive to complete things
might make you seem lesser.

I loved you and hoped
you'd find joy in the light—
but you only tuned in
your voice born of spite.
you thought your own thoughts,
the whispers so mean,
then you believed
that voice...it was me.

I'm no longer laughing
I truly am done,
I gave you my love
and now you've got none.
the war that you waged
to make me comply—
enjoy it now, arsehole—
that voice wasn't mine.

>   I'm now going to live
>   a life free without you,
>   no more will you steal
>   the happiness I knew.
>   I'm sick of you strangling
>   every ounce of my joy,
>   your thoughts always quashing
>   every part of my soul.
>   you thought your own thoughts
>   then decreed they were me,
>   I'm done—it's over
>   now please let me be."

the door clicked behind her,
the damage was done—
and still he stood there,
with blood on his hands.

>   I know what she thought,
>   he said with a growl,
>   she's not going to leave me
>   that isn't allowed.
>   I know what she wanted,
>   she's just acting odd,
>   maybe it's something
>   that was said by her squad.

the voice in his head
piped up, bold and sure,
talking his logic and
calming the storm:

> you know it's her fault,
> she'll be back and she'll grovel,
> she'll realise her mistake,
> take blame for the struggle.
> she'll say that she's sorry,
> she caused all this mess—
> she knows she's unstable,
> she knows she's a wreck.
> she'll have to be punished
> as she said it's abuse
> she twisted your kindness,
> and repaid it with grief.

so he waits by the door
and waits for the phone
but she's really done now;
she prefers being alone.
her body was broken,
her mind torn apart,
but her spirit grows stronger—
and she's healing her heart.

MAIN CHARACTER SYNDROME

you needed me to feel so small,
so you could feel you're ten feet tall.
you couldn't stand me rising high—
you'd rather clip my wings than fly.
each time I climbed, you stayed below,
and tried to stop my upward flow.
you tugged the rungs from under me,
afraid of what the world might see.

you stole the credit I had earnt,
dismissing all the ways I learnt.
you said my wins were thanks to you,
though none of that was ever true.
you cast yourself the central sun—
the axis praise would circle on
to feed your need to feel supreme,
no room for me, no space to dream.

you would not let me own my grief,
you stole my pain, beyond belief.
my tears, my wounds, my breaking soul
became your tale, you claimed control.
why was it hard to let me claim
a private space beyond your game?
why must the things that made me *me*
become your claim, your property?

you questioned every choice I made—
the clock I hung, each painting laid.
you swore my thoughts were not my own,
my very self was overthrown.
each step I took, each joy, each pain,
you twisted for your selfish gain.
I breathed, and somehow that, too, bled
into the script inside your head.

yet still I climb toward the sky,
while you stay stuck and question why.
it wasn't glory I pursued,
just simple joy you'd long subdued.
you called it selfish when I grew—
as if my light diminished you.
you couldn't thrive without a fight—
unless you'd robbed me of my light.

and still I ask—what did you gain
from turning triumph into pain?
why must your worth be bought with mine,
as though I stole your right to shine?
you needed me beneath your feet
to feel your broken world complete.
you'd rather see me torn apart
than let me thrive with open heart.

NEVER

friendship isn't hurt,

and friendship isn't pain.

friendship isn't lies—

      or threats—

      or ultimatums.

friendship is supporting,

even though you may not agree.

I was your friend.

but you were never a friend to me.

CARROTS

he dangled a holiday—
a fun trip abroad,
one day—someday.
not immediately—
but later,
if she made sure not to upset him.
if her tone stayed sweet,
if her timing was right,
if she asked for nothing
he didn't already plan to give.

he painted scenes in vivid colour:
whisky flights, speedboat rides,
a helicopter to windswept isles—
so long as she smiled
and only approached him
with kindness.

he spoke at length
about keeping her "hamsters" at bay—
those noisy thoughts,
the ones that remembered
what he'd said and done.
no dredging up the past,
no reliving scenes
that made him uncomfortable.
if she kept things light—
then maybe

he'd take her to dinner.
maybe he'd smile.

he whispered of a castle
built from the cloud of her own longing—
a sanctuary just out of reach,
if only she'd forget his past words,
let them melt
like dreams in the mist.

he made her dream of a future
where anything was possible.
he fed her visions,
just enough to keep her still.
a little more patience,
a little more compliance,
a little more smiling on cue—
and maybe,
just maybe,
he'd let her have something
that looked like kindness.

she learned not to ask.
not to press.
not to question
why the gifts never arrived.
the promises faded like fog at dawn,
and still she waited—
thinking if she were good enough,

quiet enough—
she might finally earn
the promises he dangled
but never meant to give.

UNFORGIVABLE

the unforgivables—
    acts truly heinous,
    inexcusable,
    and unpardonable.

to steal affection from another,
then blame the plundered.

to silence a voice,
born from wounds you inflicted
as if their hurt holds no worth.

to claim another's tragedy,
your minor imposition eclipsing their devastation.

to demand the blame bends from you,
    the instigator,
    the main actor,
    and the executioner.

you will never be forgiven
for what you did,
then dared to demand I ignore it.

CREATIVE VAMPIRISM

he threw money at those who created—
faking his support to conceal what he craved
he lacked an artistic voice of his own,
unable to write, couldn't sing or draw.
he had tried—gave up—always failed;
his soul, a hollow where colours drained
he didn't want beauty to stir his joy
he wanted a way in, so he could exploit
he latched onto artists to drain them dry
his support came laced with demands sky-high.
he took their profits, their praise, their palettes
a bloodsucker gorging on gifted talent.
they did the work, he claimed their profits
siphoned their earnings to give him comfort
and when they dared to speak or flee,
he curled his lip and spat with glee:
you wouldn't be here if it wasn't for me

THE FEAR INSIDE

the worms of fear, they burrow deep,
within a mind where shadows creep.
they squirm and writhe, a constant dread,
in damaged thoughts, profoundly fed.

ever checking, always poised,
a vigilance that's never paused.
scanning gentle breezes light,
for shifts that signal coming night.
a subtle change in air's soft sigh,
foretells a storm beneath the sky.
they must stay far ahead, you see,
of unpredictable calamities.

each step a strategy within a game,
within a room, with him, the same
she scanned for exits, watched the signs,
and chose her seat along the lines.
always kept a watchful eye
across from where volcanoes lie.
a clear, unbroken view to run,
should panic rise or danger come.

the backs of doors—a quick fast scan,
she checked for locks, a cautious plan.
for he, unbidden, just walks on through,
invading spaces, fresh and new.

a jarring jolt—a phone's harsh hum,
her stomach twisting, coming numb.
anxiety's grip, a tightening knot—
was it a question—or a shot?
a whispered jest, a cutting jab?
the screen—a fuse, about to snap,
a detonating light, so near,
if ever viewed, confirming fear.

but deeper still, the silence reigns,
where whispered doubts tie psychic chains.
a constant hum of what might be,
a future built on agony.

each time he glanced, a judgment held,
each passing moment, fear compelled.
his world inside—a hostile place,
reflected in her pale face.
and sleep—a fragile, fleeting grace,
haunted by what time can't erase.
for even dreams become a stage,
where fear still turns another page.

the worms of fear, they will not rest—
a life consumed, forever stressed.

DUFFTOWN

a world away in Dufftown,
outside the Co-op on Fife Street,
just after I'd bought
a bottle of water and pain medication
(that Glenfiddich tour had been awesome),
the kraken of fear wrapped its tentacles
around the world and grabbed me—
pinning me in place,
preventing movement,
squeezing the oxygen
from my lungs.

oh my god.
he has found me.

half the world away—
and a bit more for good measure—
a white VW Transporter
sat across the road
from the milksheds
where I was staying—
idling.

same model.
same year.
parked there, waiting—
like a troll beneath a bridge,
engine humming.
menacing.
familiar.
unsafe.

everything inside me screamed *run,*
but my legs were stuck
held fast by the kraken's unyielding grasp.

then—
the neurons clicked,
zapping the kraken,
forcing its retreat.
its tentacles slid free,
releasing me.

my heart drummed,
stuttered, restarted.
breath whooshed back—
oxygen and carbon dioxide
finally mixing again.

it can't be him.
I'm half a world away,
drinking whisky.
he's still stuck in a suburb,
losing money,
half a world away—
and then some.

not here.
not watching.

he can't be.
not here.

CRUMBLING REALITY

she questioned everything
told her memory was faulty
making up conversations
that she remembered clearly

could not work out if her reality was true
or if she was falling apart internally

she replayed moments repeatedly
looking for cracks in her own certainty
losing trust in her own instincts
wondered if silence meant guilty

she was unsure
if she was descending into insanity

she started saving screens
told her mind was failing
recording in her diary
thoughts she's had daily
her mind crumbling under weighty
words of others

she said "I remember it this way"
and told "you always assume things"
she folded in, afraid of her voice
began reviewing her thoughts before thinking

questions reverberating around her skull
"you're not well, you're not in control"

not sure of anything
confusion reigning
over the disintegrating
hold on her memory

was she falling into madness
or was someone distorting time and space
for their own purpose.

RECLAIMED

SAFE

she built walls around her heart—
shaped bricks from the mud
formed by dirt
her tears had fallen on,
bonded together with
the cement of her will
she scraped from her inner self,
reinforced
with a mesh of titanium
forged from the resilience
mined in the depths
of her soul.

she built a fortress around her mind—
high and impenetrable,
guarded by silent sentinels
refusing entry to any thoughts
designed to damage.
within—she nurtures newborn
seeds of trust and belief,
holding them close to
allow them room to grow.

she tends them in safety,
watering her fragile hope
with cleansing tears of past,
shielding against storms of doubt,

while she builds—
not just walls of stone and steel,
but a sanctuary where
the fragile and the fierce
exist
and safety allows
her soul to heal.

YOUR NAME IS LIAR

you once had a name
one I would use happily
to describe a lover, a friend,
someone I had absolute trust in
who I would have—
at one stage—
supported through anything
but not now—
never.

my mouth refuses
to utter a single syllable
of your name's construction
my brain seizes with disillusionment
if even the slightest shape
of the letters is viewed
your name has ceased being:
lover.
friend.
confidant.
trustworthy.
you.

your name became a loaded gun—
a flood of bad memories
triggered by a simple
four letter word.

your name has been replaced
by the adjectives and verbs of your actions
no longer a proper noun
no longer associated
with good,
with memories,
with anything of that time.

your name is Liar.
for the words you enunciated
throughout our connection
based on delusions, confusions,
and ego.
for the bullshit you wrote
and spoke
that were nothing
but hateful mistruths.

your name is Pain.
for the knife you struck
when I wasn't looking,
filled with poison
that destroyed
my beliefs,
stole my hope, and
my ability to trust—
even in myself.

your name is Hate.
for the dark shadows
you cast over every memory,
consuming and destroying.
for the calculated construction
of smears—
undermining me,
trying to take me down
even while I still believed in you.

your name is Abuse.
for the lights you lit
along the path we walked—
filled with noxious gas.
for the history we created
even as you erased it
while were still walking it
for the lies,
and the pain,
and the hate.

you had a name—
but it has been struck out,
deleted and overwritten.
I have buried it.
you are only your actions now—
own them.

CLARITY

our friendship didn't fall apart
because I envied your new partner—
though I imagine it was easier to create that reality
than face the mirror of your own cruelty.

our friendship didn't die quickly and abruptly—
it was already in a last final throe,
flailing on the wharf—gasping for oxygen—
when you told me you had finally
found someone that could "put up with you."

our friendship died from small cuts:
disrespecting me as a person
cruel jokes about my intelligence
all those times I tried to talk with you
about things that were hurting—
you threw them back at me
said they were my problem.
if I didn't like it then I needed to choose:
if I wanted to be your friend,
I had to let it go—ignore your actions.

our friendship died long before
I realised it needed a funeral,
I was mourning its passing—
months before it had no heartbeat.
it was a zombie—
only I kept it moving,

instead of laying it to rest
visiting it with flowers
on the occasions it needed remembering.

our friendship died months before—
you just decided not to tell me,
stealing my affection and time,
even though you no longer respected
my voice, my care, or my person.
I kept showing up
long after you had abandoned me
you said nothing—
because you knew what silence could steal—
you wanted me to give
while avoiding reciprocity.

clarity has found me—
time and introspection showing
rot that had existed
from the very beginning,
beneath what I had called love.
you buried the friendship long ago—
and I have let it go.

no flowers on the gravesite.
no eulogies spoken in silence.
just a death—
not worth remembering.

GOD OF THE ABYSS

he strides through his dominion
within the abyssal depths of his own mind.
blind to the putrescence decay,
his thoughts drip like maggots within his ruined soul.
his psyche pock-marked and deeply crevassed,
evidence of decades of malevolent discontent.
subconsciously comprehends that *he* is the nightmare,
concealing his true form from others—
and from himself.

his world embodies shadowy entwined mazes
threaded together by a labyrinth of lies—
created by deceit.
continuously tweaking and plucking, moving and cutting,
he manipulates all within his sphere.
certain of his own superiority,
he disregards reality in favour of his own
delusions and fantasies.
compellingly fervent that his dishonesty is truth
and all that disagree are crazy in their beliefs.

he wears his skin suit comfortably,
fitting cleanly and snugly over the decomposing obscenity.
constructed from the ruined spirits
of those that once trusted,
unfortunate souls that resisted his influence.
he took what he coveted—
leaving empty shells littering the dark corners of his mind,

discarded and forgotten.
kind eyes, charismatic smile,
a mask of gentle compassion—
disguising injurious intent.

he espies a wounded dove,
hurt by previous encounters with toxicity—
he internally smirks—aroused.
false empathy and concern seduce her,
enticing her towards his dark twisted desires.
he drips words of care and kindness,
masking the oozing acid that will corrode her from within.
fabricating a sense of safety,
a cage to keep her in,
manipulation uniting them—
for he is her soul mate.

he wants her close—to love him as he is—
but does not understand love as he cannot feel anything.
he fears she will eventually see the monster within—
his loathsome, abhorrent form—
and abandon him.
limiting what she can see of his cruelty,
he mixes light and dark until she blames internally.
inexplicable flips of his personality,
anger from nothing—
deliberate pain—
if only she would be nice.

incomprehensible contortions distort her mind,
her hold on what is true and false stutters.
he spins new tethers by complementing falsely,
nurturing a reliance on him to save her from herself.
her occasional slips infuriate—
can't she see he's only punishing her
so she learns not to anger him.
he is right and just;
she needs help to understand her failings—
he hurts only because he cares.

disguising his hate as empathy, lies as certainty,
pain as love, control as necessity.
promises made and never kept;
word given then denied—
he controls the light;
she receives only what he allows.
she attempts to fly,
and he draws her back in with promises of change
and past happiness.
trapped in his web,
he ruthlessly hacks her wings,
each feather torn out a reminder of her unworthiness.

he—is God.
and he will not be denied.
only he defines what truth is,
reality is his alone to design.
the corrupted degradation of his soul,

decayed ethics and morals—
worship blindly or be destroyed.
his attempt to constrain rips a hole in the chimaera,
and she glimpses the nightmare atrocity.
the rotting corpulent body manipulating entangled deceits,
the never-ending mazes within the bottomless abyss.

her perception of him altered by the unspeakable truth,
unaware of her pending ruin,
he attacks—
mercilessly.
he tears the flesh of her soul,
ripping out what he desires for himself,
draining her last remnants of self-worth.
discarding her decimated mind,
he mocks her to his devotees;
insanity has engulfed her—beware.
his deception builds
on the lies of the mistruths of his treachery.
for he is God—
venerate and fear him.

HOLLOW ECHOES

she was lost in the confusion,
certainty slipping through her fingers
as reality had become unnavigable—
direction arrows lost in fog,
and nothing pointing the same way.

she used to believe him—
believe in him—
believe everything he ever told her.

she tried to find meaning
in the madness,
cast lines out and only caught rubbish—
all the things that never made sense.

she realised she couldn't tell
what was real anymore—
his world was a blur:
delusions spoken as fact,
half-truths dressed as reality.

they had built a foundation
with a house of cards,
layered with promises and projections,
teetering and toxic.
she kept hoping stability
would come with time,
but it was built on quicksand—

the more she tried to stand firm,
the deeper it sank.

it was always going to fail.

she was trapped in a miasma,
circling the same ghosts:
the words he said,
and then didn't say—
the actions he took,
indecipherable and foreign.
she had become a shadow of herself,
wandering through a mystery
she didn't ask to be part of.

she kept asking—
who are you, really?
the question echoed in the abyss.
the version of him she once cared for,
and the versions—
so many versions—
that he acted on so many stages,
blurred together
until she could no longer tell
which was closest to the truth—
or if there was any truth at all.

that's when it hit her:
    she did not know him.
    and she never would.

not because she didn't try.

she asked questions
met with silence and obfuscation.
queries for clarification
answered with demands to let it go.
requests to explain why
what he said last month
didn't match what he was saying today—
met with accusations:
    she was bullying,
    misinterpreting,
    twisting his words.

he was always hiding—
behind charm,
behind misdirection,
behind layers of smoke and mirrors.
the self he showed her was
    shifting,
    elusive,
    a mask worn over a mask,
    over a mask.

she stopped trying to find the truth
in the madness
found peace in surrendering
any need to understand
as she could not think in distortion.

some truths are not just hidden—
they, like him,
are hollow echoes in the dark.

NO REGRETS

when death finally finds me—
far later, I hope, in my years—
and my life runs in flashes
of a reel of a movie I starred in,
I'll remember the joy:
the comforting embraces of my children,
my family gathered around making
silly jokes at each other,
my father's voice on old holidays,
long friendships forged through time,
the road trips and revelations,
the quiet, surprising forms of love,
care and companionship.

but when the scenes shift past
the crooked trig station
on Mt Twynam's skyline,
the little red hut named for Valentine,
or the sapphire depth of Lord Howe's tides,
you won't be there.

you had won a role in my movie,
gave an outstanding performance
in your audition,
but your CV was full of movies
that you were never actually in.
you were an actor playing a part

while speaking from your own script
within the frame of the lens
but never truly in it—
not even a background character
with no spoken words
as that would have required
your actual presence.

I'm not rewriting the script.
I'm simply ignoring the parts
that never truly belonged,
leaving them on the cutting room floor,
removing the scenes that contained
a production that was
inauthentic and wrong.

so, when the reaper comes,
and the final credits roll—
full of names that mattered—
yours won't be among them.
not as a cameo.
not in the fine print.

you didn't do anything
that deserves recognition.

BALANCED

time does not dissolve
actions that break—
as if pouring threats and undermining
into a bucket of solvent
could absolve you
of what you did—
that waiting months,
or even years,
would make the blood you spilt
any less red.

the balance of our connection
hinged on the fulcrum of my tolerance,
heavily skewed towards focussing
on the weight
lightly applied to
the so-called good side,
while blinding myself
to the kilograms you kept shovelling
onto the loaded side of bad.

each promise broken,
each word not kept,
every threat received—
weighed so much more
than the funny puns
or the basic compliments
you never meant.

the occasional meet-up
where you bought whisky
does not erase the demands
on what I was allowed to say.

my person was being crushed
by my inability to see
the growing imbalance.

I kept recalibrating,
desperate to find equilibrium—
filling the good with lies
I told myself,
excuses for why you were doing it—
the blame you placed on me
and I absorbed,
while you piled on more tons
with every dismissive shrug,
every time you smirked
when I kept ignoring your actions.

did you think I would find forgiveness—
ignore my own inner voice
after you did what you did
and said what you said?

would you have accepted your actions
if I had done them to you?

you wouldn't have lasted
a single moment
under the weight that became my burden.

time does not erase
hurt that was inflicted—
the good does not balance
the mountain of ill-deeds
created and thrown at me.

the scales are broken now—
and all that is left
is silence.

DROWNED BY INDIFFERENCE

one inviolable rule when in the water:
stay in a group, look out for your friends
you have to be able to rely on them.
I kept checking, raising my head
seeing if you were still swimming
keeping close enough if you needed assistance

but my trust was misplaced.
as I admired coral and sunken timbers
you swam away—
even though you knew I was injured.

I was left in the blue,
between colourful fish and the far horizon
you left me out there—
broken.

I floated—endless sky above,
as the ocean pulled me under,
seagulls cried like distant ghosts,
then silence—as the sea swallowed me.

not once did you think of me.
never did you look back,
even when I called for help,
you left me out there—
drowning.

so—I learnt:
I could only ever rely on me;
you didn't care enough
to even think to save me.

I found the strength to swim—
somewhere out there
between the island and the horizon.

when you finally came into view,
I wore a smile over my grimace—
prey should never show a predator
its wounds.

I grinned when I wanted to cry.
hugged when I felt abhorrence.
laughed when I wanted to flee.
buried my hurt deep.

I pretended—
to save myself from destruction.

never again could I trust someone
who didn't care
that I had drowned.

THE CLIFF FACE ABOVE THE SEA

I was holding onto the weeds
on the cliff face above the sea
as I was forced to choose my reality.
as the roots start pulling loose
I needed to make the choice
whether I would believe in you - or believe me.

my feet they found a ledge
a solid place inside my head
I had selected the only thing that had made sense.
I seized the truth with open hands
no longer lost in shifting sands
and pulled myself up to safety from the edge.

I walked away through the scrub
never once did I look back
at the crumbling cliff face high above the sea.
I had come so close to dying
by refusing to see your lying
but in the end—I had made the choice of me.

CONTROLLED

the heart of the brumby will always be wild

always will it wish to run free,

although you think you have broken its spirit

you'll never control it completely.

you tried your hardest to destroy its nature

with the whip, and the harness and reins.

as the light slowly dimmed from its eyes

the more nasty and cruel you became.

as you limited its ability to walk the world freely,

cut off from its family and friends.

you thought you had rights to its being—

that its freedom should bend to your hand.

but the heart of the brumby will always be wild

while you thought its fight was dead,

it dreamed of the mountains and wide-open spaces

in the safe space inside of its head.

there will come a day you believe you're triumphant
when the brumby will baulk at your being
as deep down inside the crushed, damaged psyche
its spirit will spark revolution.

as the heart of a brumby will always be wild
and throw off the chains you designed.
there is no one alive in this world to control
a brumby who has chosen to be free.

MARKED BY YOUR HATRED

you built a personality by taking bits from other people
like random Lego bricks from different sets—hoping
that the construction of an edifice of non-matching
ideologies would somehow make you more attractive.
while stealing those reflections you left behind
grey blocks of your own damaged character
that you could not look at or acknowledge
slipping them in amongst the others' collections
then pointing them out and shaming them for having them.

I was marked by you as a being you could borrow from
slipping your hand inside my person and taking
pieces of me that you admired and coveted
because you needed me much more than I ever needed you.
you kept me in your periphery, out of reach but always near
so you could create my personality out of all those parts
that you did not want to take responsibility
the loathing of your character from deep within
given as a present that I never once asked for or wanted.

I was marked by your hatred, dragged into servitude
moulded into vessel to pour your disgust into—exposing
all the broken pieces piled up within the container
you had hidden them in—so that others would hate me
as much as you hated and you could feel better
their aversion was aimed away from where you were located
avoiding the consequences of the words of your behaviour
you needed me to be the persona you created
just so you could hate yourself from afar.

I MOURNED YOU

I mourned you
late at night in the moonlight,
when a silly pun was spoken,
or I read a stupid meme about whisky.
I mourned our friendship.

you were a cirrus cloud in the height of spring—
beautiful, but shapeless.
a will-o'-wisp in the marshes amongst
the shadows beneath Ginini—
luring me in—only to lose me.
or a fog over the creek near my house in winter—
you had form,
but nothing I could grasp onto.

the version I had of you
was built from puzzle fragments:
the warmth of a hand you never offered,
a voice on a call you never made,
a name spoken by others
in a language I was not taught.

people asked who I had lost.
I could not answer clearly.
a shadow?
a friend?
a stranger I thought had my back?

how do you say goodbye to someone
without any form to cremate?

so—I wept.
and I grieved—
I grieved the version you sold me,
the one you forged out of compliments and silence
and the lies that blossomed like art pieces.
I swallowed it—
believing in depth
where there was only performance.

I imagined something real,
because you mirrored back what I had hoped for.
but all I ever touched
was smoke—
and the knives that you had hidden.

you never owned that damage you wrought—
only redirected it,
weaponised your wounds,
then played the victim while I bled.

and still—I mourned.
not for *you*.
but for the time I can't reclaim.
for caring for winds I could never hold.
for trusting in an illusion.

I didn't lose you.
how could I—when you never showed up?

I lost things you never held;
    my hopes.
    my dreams.
    my belief in myself.
I grieved my innocence, shredded by indifference.

I grieved what never was,
because one cannot love
a figment of someone else's imagination.

I mourned you.
I grieved for you.

but I do not miss *you*.

BLIND

I wandered blind through the storms created in his mind.

> an echo of myself within the hollowness of his soul.
> he cloaked me in kindness—cold, calculated—
> fed me silence dressed as sanctuary.

I believed him.

> I bled for his smiles, twisted for his warmth.
> each word he whispered—poison in my veins,
> each touch—a tether, each promise—a prison.

He called it love.

> but love does not bruise the soul and steal memory.
> love does not sculpt you from pain and call it devotion.
> it was never love. It was exploitation.

He built a house of lies and named it forever.

> painted guilt on my bones, my voice unheard.
> he cracked the mirror of my mind
> then told me I was the broken one.

But something in me flagged the confusion.

> a flicker in the static. a glimmer of truth in the chaos.
> the dream of who I had been
> before his shadows consumed my sunshine.

I gathered the pieces of me—defiant.

    Stitched myself back together in moonlight.
    I remembered the sound of truth
    and it burnt in me like a bonfire.

He threw hate as I rose — for bullies are weak

    the pedestal shattered from beneath the illusion.
    I saw him then—not god, not power, not love—
    just a crumbling shell of fear and hunger.

I would not—could not—accept it anymore.

    released from the shackles he had given me
    unbound by his opinion of who I was
    I carried the light he was unable to kill.

SMILE

I was smashed into a million shards,
left picking up the broken parts.
the marks you left remain here still—
etched on my heart, my soul atilt.

but I will find my joy once more,
a light that rises from my core.
my soul rebuilt, my spirit mends—
I've learnt I rise, I do not bend.

the deepest cracks I filled with gold,
a masterpiece these scars now hold.
my pieces fused, my spirit whole —
more beautiful now than what you stole.

I'll smile beneath the morning light,
a gerbera, vibrant, yellow, bright.
I'll stand with truth beneath the moon,
and know I will not break too soon.

I'll dance beneath the silver rain,
my joy released from every chain.
I'll run into the storm and grin,
as thunder rolls and heavens spin.

I'll greet each soul with warmth and grace,
leave kindness shining in my place.
I'll climb the heights that call to me,
and lift up those who cannot see.

we all deserve a love that stays,
a heart that meets us in our maze.
we need a hand, a steady guide,
a voice that's soft, a strength beside.

I found myself within the dust.
survival is not silence—it's trust.
I found my voice. I chose to speak.
I'm not ashamed. I am not weak.

though once I broke and hit the floor,
I rose again—and something more.
a phoenix forged from your destruction—
you fell beneath my own eruption.

SURVIVAL

IS NOT

SILENCE

AFTERWARD

Leaving a toxic relationship is like awakening from being smothered and gasping for breath. The critical time in the months after as you are struggling with cognitive dissonance and thoughts that maybe you were completely wrong, balanced by the ever continuing revelations that what you knew about someone – what they had told you – was never true, and you had spent (in some cases) years with a person that you actually had no idea at all who they were at all. You are left holding the cremated ashes of someone that never existed.

It is a very difficult thing to come to terms with, and you can spend far too much time trying to understand the incomprehensible. For those still struggling, I recommend *Dr Ramani* – she has a podcast and several books addressing gaslighting, narcissism and toxic people – and more importantly steps you can take to heal yourself.

I had not planned to write this book; I had thought that I had finished with this subject after *toxic/empathy* had vomited itself onto the pages and got out of my head. True to form though, toxic people can resurface, unwanted and unlooked-for in your life – in a way this book was the result of that. It started writing itself in my head on the walks I do daily, beating at the insides of my skull, demanding to be freed. I opened my laptop and it almost wrote itself.

Marked By Your Hatred I do hope is the final book in this part of my journey – but one never knows what life will hand them. Be gentle, read, walk, skip and dance – you are here and that is to be celebrated.

Much Love,

J.L. Herald

N●TES

Marked by your Hatred is a collection of poems that has been supported by research and discussions regarding emotional and psychological abuse, as well as in-depth research into what used to be known as the 'Cluster B' personality disorder types: narcissist, sociopath, and psychopath.

These have been more recently collapsed into a disorder known as anti-social personality disorder (ASPD) - a mental health condition characterized by a long-term pattern of disregard for and violation of the rights of others. The key characteristics of individuals with ASPD:

Disregard for the rights of others: consistently violate the rights of others, whether through deceit, aggression, or disregard for social norms.

Lack of empathy and remorse: often show little or no empathy for the feelings or suffering of others and may not feel guilt or regret for their actions.

Manipulative and exploitative behaviour: may use charm, deception, or intimidation to get what they want from others.

Impulsivity and irresponsibility: may act without thinking, make poor decisions, and fail to fulfill obligations.

Irritability and aggressiveness: may be prone to angry outbursts and physical altercations.

PSYCHOLOGICAL THEMES

Marked By Your Hatred covers many psychological themes associated with toxic relationships, and emotional and psychological abuse. Some of these are obvious in the poems i.e. Lighting of the Gas specifically addresses gaslighting, others may not be as obvious, so I have listed them here for completeness:

Theme: Psychological Splitting

Also known as dichotomous thinking or black-and-white thinking, involves the inability to reconcile conflicting positive and negative qualities within oneself, leading to extreme and unstable perceptions. It is a psychological defence mechanism in which an individual struggles to reconcile the positive and negative aspects of themselves into a cohesive sense of identity. Instead, they mentally divide these traits, projecting the parts they consider "bad" onto a separate, internal persona. In their own mind, this other self carries out the harmful actions, while their idealised self remains blameless.

By splitting off their negative behaviours, the individual can downplay or completely disown responsibility. When confronted, they may genuinely feel as though they are being accused of something they didn't do—because, in their mind, *it wasn't them*. This psychological divide becomes a convenient shield from accountability, but one that ultimately distorts both truth, selfhood, and reality. It also can feed into gaslighting.

Poems: Gemini; Testing; Dichotomy of Reality; Expectations

Theme: DARVO

*DARVO—Deny, Attack, and Reverse Victim and Offender—*is a common manipulative tactic used by abusers to avoid accountability and destabilize their victims. Many of the poems in *Marked by Your*

Hatred either explicitly portray this pattern or illustrate its effects on the speaker.

Poems: Non-Fiction; Betrayed by Body Language; I'm the Crazy One; Main Character Syndrome; Enough...No more

Theme: Pathological Projection

Where someone attributes their own unwanted thoughts, feelings, or behaviours to someone else—is a prominent psychological mechanism explored throughout *Marked by Your Hatred*. The person projects their guilt, shame, and rage onto another person, blaming them for emotions or actions they cannot acknowledge in themselves.

Poems: I'm the Crazy One; Main Character Syndrome; Astral Stalking; Marked by Your Hatred; Enough...No more

Theme: Cognitive Dissonance

The psychological discomfort caused by holding conflicting beliefs, values, or perceptions—is a major undercurrent in *Marked by Your Hatred*. Many poems reflect the speaker's attempt to reconcile what they were told with what they felt, what they experienced with what they were made to believe. This internal contradiction is central to the emotional damage caused by gaslighting, manipulation, and coercive control.

Poems: Non-Fiction; I'm the Crazy One; Broken Marble

Theme: Abuse Conditioning / Intermittent Reinforcement

The process by which a victim is gradually trained—psychologically and emotionally—to tolerate, normalize, or even anticipate abuse. One of the most effective tools for this conditioning is intermittent reinforcement, where positive experiences (love, approval, affection) are sporadically and unpredictably given, often between episodes of criticism, silence, or cruelty. This can be through the abuser being pleasant one day, and then cruel, dismissive, or unresponsive (silent treatment) the next, which leads to the victim questioning whether they have done something to cause this change. This behaviour is deliberate and manipulative.

Over time, the brain becomes conditioned to crave the reward, despite the pain surrounding it—a trauma bond. This mirrors psychological experiments where animals or humans respond most compulsively to unpredictable rewards.

Poems: Testing; Enough...No More

Theme: Loss of Autonomy

The gradual or sudden erosion of a person's ability to make independent decisions, assert boundaries, or maintain a clear sense of self. In abusive relationships, this loss is often systematically engineered through emotional manipulation, coercion, and gaslighting. The victim's own thoughts, preferences, actions—even their reality—are overridden by the abuser's imposed narrative. The victim attempting to reassert their own authentic self – state their thoughts, preferences, and beliefs - are told they are wrong or even delusional.

One significant dimension of this is the projection of self by the abuser: the abuser attempts to overwrite the victim's identity with a distorted reflection of their own needs, insecurities, thoughts, beliefs, or shame. This involves not only projecting their own negative traits onto the victim (e.g., calling them manipulative or unstable) but also shaping the victim's behaviour and beliefs until the victim no longer trusts their own instincts or desires. Over time, the victim may feel disconnected from their former self, unsure of their preferences, and afraid to act without approval or permission. This internal captivity is a hallmark of long-term psychological abuse.

Poems: Enough...No More; Expectations; Lighting of the Gas; Safe; Main Character Syndrome; No Wasn't an Option; Controlled

Theme: C-PTSD

Complex Post Traumatic Stress Disorder (C-PTSD) is a mental health condition that arises from prolonged or repeated exposure to traumatic events, particularly those involving interpersonal harm, such as domestic violence, and emotional and psychological abuse. Unlike standard PTSD, which often results from a single traumatic incident, C-PTSD encompasses a broader range of symptoms that reflect the enduring impact of sustained trauma.

Key Symptoms of C-PTSD

Symptom	Description
Re-Experiencing The Trauma	Flashbacks, nightmares, intrusive thoughts, or intense physical reactions to reminders of the trauma.
Avoidance	avoiding places, people, activities, or thoughts that remind them of the trauma.
Hyperarousal/ Hypervigilance	Feeling constantly on edge, easily startled, irritable, or having difficulty sleeping.
Emotional Dysregulation	Difficulty managing emotions, leading to intense anger, sadness, or emotional numbness.
Negative Self-Perception	Persistent feelings of worthlessness, shame, or guilt.
Interpersonal Difficulties	Challenges in forming or maintaining relationships due to distrust or detachment.
Dissociation	Experiences of feeling disconnected from oneself or the surrounding environment.
Physical Symptoms	Chronic pain, gastrointestinal issues, or other somatic complaints without a clear medical cause.

Poems: Many Watchers; Dufftown; Psychosomatic; Unwanted; I'm the Crazy One; Safe; Expectations

About the Author

JL Herald grew up in Canberra, Australia and has a Bachelor of Social Sciences from the University of Canberra. The mother of six mainly now adult children, she lives with her 2 cats, Sox and Eevee, and her beagle Sherlock.

Her first book *toxic/empathy* was published in 2024, and she re-published her great (x4)-grandfathers Alexander Herald's poetry book *Amusements of Solitude* in 2024.

www.ingramcontent.com/pod-product-compliance
Lightning Source LLC
Chambersburg PA
CBHW072335300426
44109CB00042B/1623